THE SPIRIT SHOULD NOT GROW OLD

A Treasury of Inspirational Quotations

by

Anita K. Tanner, MSW

Printed in the United States of America

First Printing, 2018

ISBN 978-1-7329306-0-5

Thornbrook Press
27665 Yvette Drive
Warren, MI 48088

CONTENTS

Foreword

From an early age, I felt inspired by quotes. I memorized them, recited them and carried them with me in my handbag. Quotes have, throughout my life, provided me with the right words when I had no words of my own.

I began collecting quotes at eleven years old when I discovered a particularly profound passage cited in a local newspaper:

> "Four things come not back:
> The spoken word
> The sped arrow
> Time past
> The neglected opportunity."

I snipped it out and kept it with me for years afterward. This single quote has had a tremendous impact on the way that I have lived—and still live—my life.

In my work as an educator in gerontology, and

as a clinical social worker working with people of all age groups in mental health and hospice settings, I have found that there is often a need and a use for good quotes.

Quotes can be used to motivate, to console, to soothe, to nudge, to encourage, to reassure, to provide food for thought and to facilitate movement in a positive direction.

Whether you are young, old, or somewhere in between, my hope is that you will be able to identify with a few of the sayings in this book and that one or two of them will help to make a difference in your life.

Life, for each of us, remains full of possibilities. It will remain that way until the day we draw our last breath. It is up to each one of us to make the most of every day we live.

— Anita K. Tanner

Outlook

"If wrinkles must be written upon our brows, let them not be upon the heart. The spirit should not grow old."

James A. Garfield
20th President of the United States

"The longer I live, the more
beautiful life becomes"

Frank Lloyd Wright
Architect

"When you get into a tight place, and everything goes against you till it seems as though you could not hold on a moment longer, never give up — for that is just the place and time that the tide will turn."

Harriet Beecher Stowe

Author and abolitionist

"Yesterday is a canceled check:
Forget it.

Tomorrow is a promissory note:
Don't count on it.

Today is ready cash:
Use it."

Edwin Bliss

Journalist and educator

"If you want to test your memory, try to remember what you were worrying about one year ago today."

E. Joseph Cossman
Entrepreneur

"Things turn out best for people who make the best out of the way things turn out."

Art Linkletter

Radio and television host

"Life does not have to be
perfect to be wonderful."

Annette Funicello
Actress

"Although the world is full of suffering,
it is also full of the overcoming of it."

Helen Keller

Social reformer and activist

"Birds sing after a storm; why shouldn't
people feel as free to delight in whatever
remains to them?"

Rose Fitzgerald Kennedy

Philanthropist and matriarch of the Kennedy family

"To me this is the first principle of life, the foundational principle, and a lesson you can't learn at the foot of any wise man: Get up! The art of living is simply getting up after you've been knocked down."

Joe Biden
47th Vice President of the United States

"It never hurts your eyesight to look
on the bright side of things."

Barbara Johnson

Literary critic

"I am incapable of conceiving infinity, and yet I do not accept finity. I want this adventure that is the context of my life to go on without end."

Simone de Beauvoir

French philosopher

"Do not go gentle into that good night,
Old age should burn and rave at close of day;
Rage, rage against the dying of the light."

Dylan Thomas
Welsh poet

"Think of all the beauty still left
around you and be happy."

Anne Frank

Diarist and victim of the Holocaust

"Youth is not entirely a time of life; it is a state of mind. Nobody grows old by merely living a number of years. People grow old by deserting their ideals. You are as young as your faith, as old as your doubt; as young as your self-confidence, as old as your fear; as young as your hope, as old as your despair."

Douglas MacArthur
General

"Let us cherish and love old age, for it is full of pleasure if one knows how to use it."

Seneca
Roman Stoic philosopher

"Very early, I knew that the
only object in life was to grow."

Margaret Fuller
Author and suffragist

"You can't help getting older, but
you don't have to get old."

George Burns
Comedian

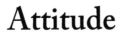

Attitude

"Years wrinkle the skin, but to give up
enthusiasm wrinkles the soul."

Samuel Ullman

Poet

"We don't stop playing because we grow old;
we grow old because we stop playing."

George Bernard Shaw
Irish playwright

"He that is discontented in one place
will seldom be happy in another."

Aesop
Greek fabulist

"If you can't change your fate,
change your attitude."

Amy Tan
Author

"The key to successful aging is to pay
as little attention to it as possible."

Judith Regan
Publisher

"There is a fountain of youth: it is your mind, your talents, the creativity you bring to your life and the lives of people you love. When you learn to tap this source, you will truly have defeated age."

Sophia Loren

Actress

"Now is no time to think of what you
do not have. Think of what you can
do with what there is."

Ernest Hemingway
Author

"Live decently, fearlessly, joyously —
and don't forget that in the long run,
it is not the years in your life, but the
life in your years that counts."

Adlai Stevenson

Politician and diplomat

"Nobody has things just as he would like them. The thing to do is to make a success with the material I have. It is a sheer waste of time and soul-power to imagine what I would do if things were different. They are not different."

Dr. Frank Crane
Presbyterian minister

"God asks no man whether he will accept life.
This is not the choice. You must take it.
The only question is how."

Henry Ward Beecher

Congregationalist minister and social reformer

"Any fact facing us is not as important as our attitude toward it, for that determines our success or failure."

"Believe that you are defeated, believe it long enough, and it is likely to become a fact. We tend to get what we expect."

Norman Vincent Peale
Best-selling author and minister

"I do the very best I know how —
the very best I can; and I mean to
keep doing so until the end."

Abraham Lincoln

16th President of the United States

"Make the most of every sense; glory in all of the pleasures and beauty which the world reveals to you."

Helen Keller

Social reformer and activist

"Whether you think you can
or think you can't — you are right."

Henry Ford

Industrialist

"Never give up.
Never give up.
Never give up."

Winston Churchill

Prime Minister of the United Kingdom

"The best way to adjust—no, ignore—most
of the negative thoughts about aging is to say
to yourself, with conviction, 'I am still the very
same person I have been all of my adult life.'
You are, you know."

Helen Hayes

Actress

"Women, I think, get better as they get older. To me, what's attractive in a woman is reflected in the way she feels about herself. She may not be the most physically beautiful woman in the world, but she becomes attractive by the way she carries herself and thinks about herself—or doesn't think about herself."

Tom Selleck

Actor

"It takes no more time to see the good side
of life than it takes to see the bad."

Jimmy Buffett

Musician

"This thing we call 'failure' is not the falling down but the staying down."

Mary Pickford

Silent movie actress and film producer

"You're never too old to become younger."

Mae West

Actress

"The mind, in addition to medicine, has powers to turn the immune system around."

Jonas Salk

Medical researcher and inventor of the polio vaccine

"When I read this I knew—as in really knew—that I was responsible for my life and that it would be the choices I made...that would determine the kind of life I had in the future. My doom was not sealed. My fate was not set. It was true that I could do nothing about what happened, but I could do everything about how I continued to react to what had happened."

Elizabeth Harper-Neeld
Author

Kindness

"No one is useless in the world who
lightens the burden of it for anyone else."

Charles Dickens
Author

"Just do what you can. It's not good enough merely to exist. Seek always to do some good somewhere...you must give some time to your fellow man. Even if it's just a little thing, do something for those who have need of help. Something for which you get no pay, but the privilege of doing it. For remember, you don't live in a world all your own. Your brothers are here, too."

Albert Schweitzer

French–German theologian and humanitarian

"The people who make a difference are not the ones with the credentials but the ones with the concern."

Max Lucado
Author

"It is a little embarrassing that, after forty-five years of research and study, the best advice I can give to people is to be a little kinder to each other."

Aldous Huxley

British author and philosopher

"The older you get, the more you realize that kindness is synonymous with happiness."

Lionel Barrymore

Actor

"I expect to pass this way but once; any good therefore that I can do, or any kindness that I can show any fellow creature, let me do it now. Let me not defer or neglect it, for I shall not pass this way again."

Etienne de Grellet

French–American Quaker missionary

"Try to be a rainbow in someone's cloud."

Maya Angelou
Writer and civil rights activist

"When I was young, I used to admire intelligent people; as I grow older, I admire kind people."

Abraham Joshua Heschel

Jewish theologian and philosopher

"You cannot do a kindness too soon,
because you never know how soon it will be
done too late."

Anonymous

"Without tenderness, a man is uninteresting."

Marlene Dietrich

German actress and singer

The Meaning of a Smile

It costs nothing
It creates much
It enriches those who receive it, without
   impoverishing those who give it
It happens in a flash
The memory of it sometimes lasts forever
There are none so rich that they can get along
   without it
There are none so poor but are richer for its
   benefits.
It creates happiness in the home
It fosters goodwill in business and is the
   countersign of friends
It is rest to the weary, daylight to the
   discouraged, sunshine to the sad
And nature's best antidote for trouble
And yet it cannot be begged, bought,
   borrowed or stolen

It is no earthly good to anyone until it is
   given away
So if in the course of the day your friends may
   be too tired to give you a smile, then why don't
   you give them one of yours?
Nobody needs a smile more than those who
   have none left to give
Smile!

Anonymous

Forgiveness

"To harbor hatred and animosity in
the soul makes one irritable, gloomy,
and prematurely old."

Berthold Auerbach

German–Jewish author

"One only must grow old to be more
forgiving; I see no fault of which
I have not been guilty myself."

Johann Wolfgang von Goethe
German author and polymath

"Forgiveness is the answer to the child's dream of a miracle by which what is broken is made whole again, what is soiled is again made clean. The dream explains why we need to be forgiven, and why we must forgive. In the presence of God, nothing stands between Him and us — we are forgiven. But we cannot feel His presence if anything is allowed to stand between ourselves and others."

Dag Hammarskjöld

First Secretary General of the United Nations

"Put from you the belief that 'I have been wronged', and with it will go the feeling. Reject your sense of injury, and the injury itself disappears."

Marcus Aurelius

Roman emperor

"Keeping score of old scores and scars,
getting even and one-upping,
always make you less than you are."

Malcolm Forbes

Entrepreneur

"Nothing is more costly,
nothing is more sterile,
than vengeance."

Winston Churchill
Prime Minister of the United Kingdom

"Anger makes you smaller, while forgiveness
forces you to grow beyond what you were."

Cherie Carter-Scott

Author and life coach

"To forgive is to overlook an offense and treat the offender as not guilty."

Zig Ziglar
Motivational speaker

"The weak can never forgive.
Forgiveness is an attribute of the strong."

Mahatma Gandhi

Activist for Indian independence

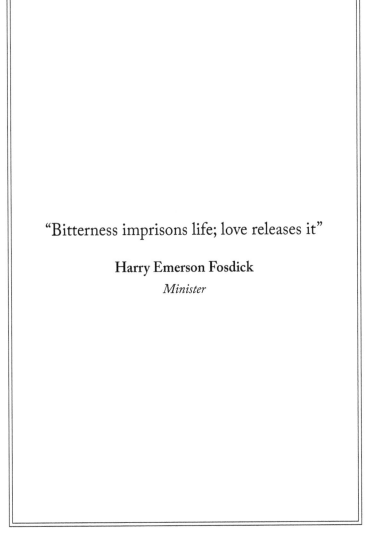

"Bitterness imprisons life; love releases it"

Harry Emerson Fosdick
Minister

"May I tell you why it seems to me a good thing to remember wrong that has been done to us? That we may forgive it."

Charles Dickens
Author

"A man can lose sight of everything else when he's bent on revenge, and it ain't worth it."

Louis L'Amour

Novelist

"How unhappy is he who
cannot forgive himself."

Publilius Syrus

Roman author

"Even God cannot change the past."

Agathon

Athenian poet and playwright

Laughter

"Savor the moments that are warm
and special and giggly."

Sammy Davis, Jr.
Entertainer

"You don't stop laughing because you grow old, you grow old because you stop laughing."

Michael Pritchard

Comedian and activist

"Humor is the shock absorber of life,
it helps us take the blows."

Peggy Noonan

Speechwriter, author, and political commentator

"There is a lot to be thankful for, if you take the
time to look. For example, in sitting here
thinking how nice it is that wrinkles don't hurt."

Anonymous

"The most wasted of all days
is one without laughter."

e e cummings

Poet and essayist

"Seven days without laughter makes one weak."

Mort Walker

Creator of the "Beetle Bailey" comic strip

"Laughter is good for everyone. We should all get a daily dose. Say 'ha, ha, ha, hee, hee, hee' out loud to get started. You shouldn't wait to be happy to laugh. Laughter makes us happy."

Annette Goodheart

Marriage, child, and family therapist

"Among those whom I like or admire,
I can find no common denominator, but
among those whom I love, I can:
All of them make me laugh."

W. H. Auden

Poet

"Jokes are legitimate coping mechanisms that offer a sense of relief in a scary situation."

Dr. Frederick Goodwin
Psychiatrist

"Age does not diminish the extreme
disappointment of having a scoop of
ice cream fall from the cone."

Jim Fiebig

Businessperson

"I've got 'Sometimers.'
Sometimes I remember and
sometimes I forget."

Spike Lee

Filmmaker and activist

"Laugh and grow strong."

Saint Ignatius of Loyola
Founder of the Jesuit Order

"A merry heart doeth good like a medicine;
But a broken spirit drieth the bones."

Proverbs 17:22

"You can't laugh and be afraid at
the same time — of anything."

Stephen Colbert
Comedian

"Look at Bob Hope. Look at Milton Berle, George Burns. Look at how long they lived. Seeing the funny side of things keeps you alive."

Phyllis Diller
Comedian

"I can't tell you his age, but when he was born the wonder drug was Mercurochrome."

Milton Berle

Comedian

Happiness

"The greater part of our happiness depends on our disposition and not on our circumstances."

Martha Washington

First Lady of the United States

"It is not the level of prosperity that makes
for happiness but the kinship of heart to heart
and the way we look at the world.
Both attitudes are within our power,
so that a man is happy as long as he chooses
to be happy, and no one can stop him."

Aleksandr Solzhenitsyn
Russian author

"If your happiness depends on what somebody else does, you have a problem."

Richard Bach

Writer

"I live by one principle: Enjoy life with no conditions! People say, 'If I had your health, if I had your money, oh, I would enjoy myself.' It is not true. I would be happy if I were lying sick in a hospital bed. It must come from the inside. That is the one thing I hope to have contributed to my children, by example and by talk: to make no conditions, to understand that life is a wonderful thing and to enjoy it, every day, to the full."

Arthur Rubinstein
Pianist

"If you want others to be happy,
practice compassion. If you want to
be happy, practice compassion."

The Dalai Lama
Tibetan Buddhist spiritual leader

"It's the moments that I stopped just to be, rather than do, that have given me true happiness."

Richard Branson

British entrepreneur and philanthropist

"Wrinkles should merely indicate where the smiles have been."

Mark Twain
Author

"The gladness of the heart is the life of man, and the joyfulness of a man prolongeth his days."

Ecclesiasticus 30:22

Purpose

"If we have our own why in life, we shall get along with almost any how."

Friedrich Nietzsche
German philosopher

"A musician must make music, an artist
must paint, a poet must write, if he
is to be ultimately at peace with himself.
What a man can be, he must be."

Abraham Maslow

Psychologist

"Your purpose in life is to find your purpose,
and then give your whole heart and soul to it."

The Buddha

"Everyone has a purpose in life.
Perhaps yours is watching television."

David Letterman

Late night host and comedian

"We all possess the thunder of pure fury and the calm breeze of tranquility. If it wasn't for tomorrow, how much would we get done today? Whatever your purpose...embrace it completely. Get lost in the clouds every now and then so you never lose sight of God's wonder."

Paul Vitale

Motivational speaker

"Our greatest legacy is not our accomplishments in life, it's what we can do to help the next generation."

Jimmy Carter
39th President of the United States

"Nothing contributes so much to tranquilize the mind as a steady purpose — a point on which the soul may fix its intellectual eye."

Mary Wollstonecraft Shelley
Author

"Where I was born and where and how I lived
is unimportant. It is what I have done with
where I have been that shall be of interest."

Georgia O'Keeffe
Painter

"To every thing there is a season, and a time to every purpose under heaven."

Ecclesiastes 3:1

"Great minds have purposes,
others have wishes."

Washington Irving
Author

"Here I am at the end of the road
and at the top of the heap."

Pope John XXIII

On being elected pope at age 77

"The measure of a life, after all, is not its duration but its donation."

Corrie ten Boom

Dutch writer and Holocaust survivor

"Here is the test to find whether your mission
on earth is finished: If you're alive, it isn't."

Richard Bach

Writer

"All things have been given to us for a purpose.
All that happens to us, including our
humiliations, our misfortunes, our
embarrassments, all is given to us
as raw material, as clay, so that
we may shape our art."

Jorge Luis Borges
Argentine writer

"I rejoice in life for its own sake. Life is no brief candle to me. It is a sort of splendid torch which I got hold of for a moment, and I want to make it burn as brightly as possible before turning it over to the next generations."

George Bernard Shaw
Irish playwright

"My story is a freedom song of struggle. It is about finding one's purpose, how to overcome fear, and stand up for causes bigger than one's self."

Coretta Scott King

Civil rights activist and wife of Dr. Martin Luther King, Jr.

Work & Leisure

"Retire? I can't spell the word.
I'd play in a wheelchair."

Keith Richards
Musician

"If you don't build your dream, someone
else will hire you to build theirs."

Dhirubhai Ambani

Indian businessman

"The man who works and is never bored is never old. Work and interest in worthwhile things are the best remedy for age. Each day I am reborn. Each day I must be reborn again."

Pablo Casals

Musician

"My favorite four letter words are 'hard work'."

John Wayne

Actor

"Work is the greatest thing in the world, so we should always save some of it for tomorrow."

Don Herold

Humorist

"Life is to be lived. If you have to support yourself, you had bloody well better find some way that is going to be interesting. And you don't do that by sitting around wondering about yourself."

Katharine Hepburn

Actress

"My favorite animal is the mule. He knows
when to stop eating and knows
when to stop working."

Harry S. Truman
33rd President of the United States

"It is not enough to be busy: so are the ants. The question is, what are you busy about?"

Henry David Thoreau
Writer

"Every individual should have the opportunity to develop the gifts which may be latent in him. Alone in that way can the individual obtain the satisfaction to which he is justly entitled; and alone in that way can the community achieve its richest flowering"

Albert Einstein

Scientist

"You've achieved success in your field when you don't know whether what you're doing is work or play."

Warren Beatty

Actor

"How would you like a job where, if you made a mistake, a big red light goes off and 18,000 people boo?"

Jacques Plante
Professional hockey player

"The phrase 'work-life balance' tells us that people think that work is the opposite of life. We should be talking about life-life balance"

Patrick Dixon

British business writer

Motivation

"Lift up your hearts. Each new hour
holds new chances for new beginnings."

Maya Angelou
Writer and civil rights activist

"Nothing is impossible, the word
itself says 'I'm possible.'"

Audrey Hepburn

Actress

"The word 'impossible' is not in my dictionary."

Napoleon Bonaparte

Emperor of France

"Dost thou love life? Then do not squander time, for that is the stuff life is made of."

Ben Franklin

American founding father

"Do not let what you cannot do
interfere with what you can do."

John Wooden
Basketball coach

"Nothing in the world can take the place of persistence. Talent will not; nothing is more common than unsuccessful men with talent. Genius will not; unrewarded genius is almost a proverb. Education will not; the world is full of educated derelicts. Persistence and determination alone are omnipotent. The slogan 'press on' has solved and always will solve the problems of the human race."

Calvin Coolidge
30th President of the United States

"Even if you're on the right track, you'll get run over if you just sit there."

Will Rogers

Humorist

"Growing old is no more than a bad habit which a busy person has no time to form."

Andre Maurois

French writer

"If life boils down to one thing, it's movement. To live is to keep moving."

Jerry Seinfeld
Comedian

"Four things come not back:
The spoken word,
the sped arrow,
time past,
the neglected opportunity."

Arabian proverb

"Behold the turtle. He only makes progress
when he sticks his neck out."

James Bryant Conant
President of Harvard University

"As soon as you feel too old to do a thing, do it."

Margaret DeLand
Novelist

"The tragedy of men is what dies
inside himself while he still lives."

Albert Schweitzer

French-German theologian and humanitarian

"There's no cap on success. The jury stays out 'til you take your last breath."

Judy Sheindlin

Television judge

"There's many a good tune
played on an old fiddle."

Samuel Butler
Author

"I get up before anyone else in my household, not because sleep has deserted me in my advancing years, but because an intense eagerness to live draws me from my bed."

Maurice Goudeket

Writer

"If you are trying to achieve, there will be roadblocks. I've had them, everybody has had them. But obstacles don't have to stop you. If you run into a wall, don't turn around and give up. Figure out how to climb it, go through it, or work around it."

Michael Jordan
Basketball player

"Teach me neither to cry for
the moon nor over spilt milk."

**Written on the library wall of
King George V of the United Kingdom**

"A man who wants to do something will find a way; a man who doesn't will find an excuse."

Proverb

"For of all sad works of tongue or pen, the saddest are these: 'It might have been!'"

John Greenleaf Whittier
Poet and abolitionist

"God gives every bird its food, but He does not throw it into the nest."

Josiah Gilbert Holland
Author

"A wise man will make more
opportunities than he finds."

Sir Francis Bacon
English statesman and philosopher

Learning

"You are never too old to set another
goal or to dream a new dream."

C. S. Lewis
Author

"Anyone who stops is old, whether at twenty or eighty. Anyone who keeps learning stays young. The greatest thing in life is to keep your mind young."

Henry Ford

Industrialist

"Old minds are like old horses; you must exercise them if you wish to keep them in working order."

John Adams

2nd President of the United States

"If in the last year you haven't discarded a major opinion or acquired a new one, check your pulse. You may be dead."

Sherrie Weaver

Writer

"Reading is to the mind what
exercise is to the body."

Joseph Addison
Poet and playwright

"Reading gives us someplace to go when we have to stay where we are."

Mason Cooley

Professor and aphorist

"One day, we will be the elders from whom our children and grandchildren learn. We must be effective in creating a lasting memory and understanding. Keep the chain of oral history going. Sit, talk, tell the story of your life and how you came to hold your points of view."

Milon Townsend
Artist

"You must learn day by day, year by year, to broaden your horizon. The more things you love, the more you're interested in, the more you enjoy, the more you're indignant about — the more you have left when anything happens."

Ethel Barrymore

Actress

"You will stay young as long as you learn, form new habits, and don't mind being contradicted."

Marie von Ebner-Eschenbach

Austrian novelist

"It wasn't until quite late in life that I discovered it is okay to say, 'I don't know.'"

W. Somerset Maugham
Writer

"Interesting people are people who are interested. Bores are people who are bored."

Anonymous

"Do not grow old, no matter how long you live. Never cease to stand like curious children before the Great Mystery into which we were born."

Albert Einstein

Scientist

"One of the secrets of life is to make stepping stones out of stumbling blocks."

Jack Penn

South African reconstructive surgeon

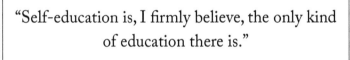

"Self-education is, I firmly believe, the only kind
of education there is."

Isaac Asimov

Science fiction author and professor

Love

"If you love somebody, tell them."

Rod McKuen

Poet

"In dreams and in love there
are no impossibilities."

János Arany
Hungarian poet

"Across the years I will walk with you — in deep, green forests; on shores of sand; and when our time on earth is through in heaven, too, you will have my hand."

Robert Sexton

Writer

"Love is everything it's cracked up to be. That's why people are so cynical about it. It really is worth fighting for, being brave for, risking everything for. And the trouble is, if you don't risk everything, you risk even more."

Erica Jong
Author

"'Nothing, so it seems to me,' said the stranger, 'is more beautiful than love that has weathered the storms of life.'"

Jerome Klapka Jerome
Writer

"The course of true love never did run smooth."

William Shakespeare

"Commitment doesn't just mean to stay with someone through thick and thin. It means to make everything work, and to help it keep on working, so each of you can trust yourself to the other in that private place, knowing that the other will do what has to be done, whatever that something is. And knowing that you always have the spiritual margin to get derailed again, and yet still grow older together, with everything intact."

Merle Shain
Author

"Age does not protect you from love. But love, to some extent, protects you from age."

Anaïs Nin
Author

"Young love is a flame; very pretty, very hot and fierce but still only light and flickering. The love of the older and disciplined heart is as coals, deep burning, unquenchable."

Henry Ward Beecher

Congregationalist minister and social reformer

"Love is patient, love is kind. It does not envy, it does not boast, it is not proud. It does not dishonor others, it is not self-seeking, it is not easily angered, it keeps no record of wrongs. Love does not delight in evil but rejoices with the truth. It always protects, always trusts, always hopes, always perseveres.
Love never fails."

1 Corinthians 13:4-8

"Love is never ending. Love is always."

Smokey Robinson
Musician

"Love is eternal."

Inscription in Abraham Lincoln's wedding ring

Friendship

"A single rose can be my garden...
a single friend, my world."

Leo Buscaglia

Professor and motivational speaker

"Just thinking about a friend makes you want to do a happy dance, because a friend is someone who loves you in spite of your faults."

Charles M. Schulz

Cartoonist

"One of the sweetest things in life:
a letter from a friend."

Andy Rooney
Radio and TV personality

"You say there is nothing to write about. Then write to me that there is nothing to write about."

Pliny the Younger

Roman author

"Blessed is the servant who loves his brother as much when he is sick and useless as when he is well and can be of service to him."

St. Francis of Assisi

"You can make more friends in two months by becoming interested in other people than you can in two years by trying to get other people interested in you."

Dale Carnegie

Lecturer and self-help author

"A real friend is one who walks in when
the rest of the world walks out."

Walter Winchell

Gossip columnist

"Old friends are the great blessing of one's later years. They have a memory of the same events and have the same mode of thinking."

Horace Walpole

British writer and statesman

"Keep the other person's wellbeing in mind when you feel an attack of soul-purging truth coming on."

Betty White
Actress

"The only record of virtue is virtue; the only way to love a friend is to be one."

Ralph Waldo Emerson

Writer

"Sometimes people say something you don't like...you let it go by, even if you really would like to choke them. By smiling, I think I've made more friends than if I was the other way."

Ella Fitzgerald

Jazz singer

"Art thou lonely, o my brother? Share thy little with another! Stretch a hand to one unfriended, and thy loneliness is ended."

William Arthur Dunkerley

Writer

"Don't walk behind me; I may not lead.
Don't walk in front of me; I may not follow.
Just walk beside me and be my friend."

Anonymous

"What a lot we lost when we stopped writing letters. You can't reread a phone call."

Liz Carpenter

Media advisor and author

Family

"At the end of your life you'll never regret not having passed one more test, not winning one more verdict, or closing one more deal. You will regret times not spent with a husband, a friend, a child, or a parent."

Barbara Bush
First Lady of the United States

"You can't do much about your ancestors, but you can influence your descendants enormously."

Anonymous

"No matter what you've done for yourself or humanity, if you can't look back on having given love and attention to your own family, what have you really accomplished?"

Lea Iacocca

Business executive

"When you look at your life, the greatest happinesses are family happiness."

Dr. Joyce Brothers

Popular psychologist

"There's nothing like a good family
when you're really up a tree."

Carolyn Hax

Advice columnist

"No matter how old a mother is, she watches
her middle-aged children for signs of
improvement."

Florida Scott-Maxwell

Writer

"When your mother asks, 'Do you want a piece of advice?' it is a mere formality. It doesn't matter if you answer yes or no. You're going to get it anyways."

Erma Bombeck
Humorist

"All mothers have intuition.
The great ones have radar."

Cathy Guisewite
Cartoonist

"When [my mother] was dying, talking to me, she said: 'Always try and be kind and nice to people. And if you do that, somebody will always speak up for you.' And I've found that to be a fact. They really do."

B. B. King
Musician

"Sooner or later, we all quote our mothers."

Sir Bernard Williams
Philosopher

"My mother was the most beautiful woman I ever saw. All I am I owe to my mother. I attribute my success in life to the moral, intellectual, and physical education that I received from her."

George Washington
1st President of the United States

"I really learned it all from my mother."

Dr. Benjamin Spock

Pediatrician and author

"Grandmothers of every race and country have a legendary role as healers. Jewish grandmothers make chicken soup; others have their own special remedies. When a child in a North American Yurok Indian tribe is ill, Grandmother goes out into the wilderness to intervene with the spirits by singing and speaking to them. Every grandmother has her own song."

Arthur Kornhaber
Physician

"I believe what we become depends on what our fathers teach us at odd moments, when they aren't trying to teach us. We are formed by little scraps of wisdom."

Umberto Eco

Italian novelist and philosopher

"Recently I was rereading one of my favorite books, Ernest Hemingway's 'The Old Man and the Sea,' and I came upon the simple line: 'The old man had taught the boy to fish and the boy loved him.' Strong and cherished feelings and memories about my father arose inside of me. My dad may never have taught me much about the fine arts and sciences, but he did teach this boy to fish. And I loved him."

Linus Mundy

Author

"My father gave me the greatest gift anyone could give another person—he believed in me."

Jim Valvano

Basketball player and coach

"When you teach your son,
you teach your son's son"

The Talmud

"Generally, the man with a good wife, or the woman with a good husband, or the children with good parents discover too late the goodness they overlooked while it was in full bloom."

James Douglas

Actor

Character

"It's not true that nice guys finish last.
Nice guys are winners before the game starts."

Mort Walker

Creator of the "Beetle Bailey" comic strip

"Character—the willingness to accept responsibility for one's own life—is the source from which self-respect springs."

Joan Didion
Novelist

"Live so that when your children think of fairness and integrity, they think of you."

H. Jackson Brown, Jr.
Author

"He has achieved success who has lived well, laughed often and loved much; who has gained the respect of intelligent men and the love of little children; who has filled his niche and accomplished his task; who has left the world better than he found it, whether by an improved poppy, a perfect poem, or a rescued soul; who has never lacked appreciation of earth's beauty or failed to express it; who has always looked for the best in others and given the best he had; whose life was an inspiration; whose memory a benediction."

Bessie A. Stanley

Essayist

"If we are strong, our character will speak for itself. If we are weak, words will be of no help."

John F. Kennedy

35th President of the United States

"Live that you would not be ashamed to sell the family parrot to the town gossip."

Will Rogers

Humorist

"A hundred years from now it will not matter
what my bank account was, the sort of house I
lived in, or the kind of car I drive...but the world
may be different because I was important
in the life of a child."

Anonymous

"Blessed is the man who can say that the boy he was would be proud of the man he is."

J. F. Burshears

Scoutmaster

"If I were asked to give what I consider the single most useful bit of advice for all humanity, it would be this: Expect trouble as an inevitable part of life and when it comes, hold your head high, look it squarely in the eye and say, 'I will be bigger than you. You cannot defeat me.'"

Ann Landers

Advice columnist

"It is almost more important how a person takes his fate than what fate it is."

Wilhelm von Humboldt

German philosopher and civil servant

"No one of good character leaves behind a wasted life — whether they die in obscurity or renown."

"It is your character, and your character alone, that will make your life happy or unhappy...and, you choose it."

John McCain

Senator

"The greatest legacy one can pass on to one's children and grandchildren is not money or other material things accumulated in one's life, but rather a legacy of character and faith."

Billy Graham

Minister and evangelist

Wisdom

"To know how to grow old is the masterwork of wisdom, and one of the most difficult chapters in the great art of living."

Henri-Frédéric Amiel

Swiss philosopher

"The whole secret of remaining young in spite of years, and even of gray hairs, is to cherish enthusiasm in oneself, by poetry, by contemplation, by charity—that is, in fewer words, by the maintenance of harmony in the soul. When everything is in its right place within us, we ourselves are in equilibrium with the whole work of God. Deep and grave enthusiasm for the eternal beauty and the eternal order, reason touched with emotion and a serene tenderness of the heart—these surely are the foundations of wisdom."

Henri-Frédéric Amiel

"The art of living successfully consists of being able to hold two opposite ideas in tension at the same time; first, to make long-term plans as if we were going to live forever; and, second, to conduct ourselves daily as if we were going to die tomorrow."

Sidney Harris

Cartoonist

"To finish the moment, to find the journey's end in every step of the road, to live the greatest number of good hours, is wisdom."

Ralph Waldo Emerson
Writer

"There are two things to aim at in life: first to get what you want and, after that, to enjoy it. Only the wisest of mankind achieve the second."

Logan Pearsall Smith

Essayist

"Wisdom is oftimes nearer when we stoop
Than when we soar."

William Wordsworth

English poet

"Just as solid rocks are not shaken by the wind, so wise men are not moved by either blame or praise."

Frank W. Boresham

Baptist minister

"The art of being wise is the art
of knowing what to overlook."

William James

Psychologist and philosopher

"A man should never be ashamed to say he has been wrong, which is but saying in other words that he is wiser today than he was yesterday."

Alexander Pope
Poet

"As for me, all I know is that I know nothing."

Socrates

Greek philosopher

Priorities

"The best things in life aren't things."

Ann Landers

Advice columnist

"Let the moment come when nothing is left but life, and you will find that you do not hesitate over the fate of your material possessions."

Eddie Rickenbacker

Fighter ace and aviation pioneer

- Keep your promises.
- Treat everyone like you want to be treated.
- Never give up on anybody. Miracles happen.
- Never deprive someone of hope. It may be all he has.
- Pray not for things, but for wisdom and courage.
- Leave everything better than you found it.
- Don't rain on other peoples' parades.
- Never waste an opportunity to tell someone you love them.

Life's Little Instruction Book

"Why hope to live a long life if we're only going to fill it with self-absorption, body maintenance, and image repair? When we die, do we want people to exclaim, 'She looked ten years younger,' or do we want them to say, 'She lived a great life'?"

Letty Cottin Pogrebin
Author

"As I grow older and older,
And totter toward the tomb;
I find that I care less and less
Who goes to bed with whom."

Dorothy Sayers

Writer and translator

"Your time is limited, so don't waste it living someone else's life. Don't be trapped by dogma — which is living with the results of other people's thinking. Don't let the noise of others' opinions drown out your own inner voice. And most important, have the courage to follow your heart and intuition."

Steve Jobs
Founder and CEO of Apple

"You only live once, but if you
do it right, once is enough."

Mae West

Actress

"If I'd known I was gonna live this long,
I'd have taken better care of myself."

Eubie Blake

Jazz pianist

"For peace of mind, resign as
general manager of the Universe."

Larry Eisenberg
Sci-fi writer

"The best doctors in the world are Doctor Diet, Doctor Quiet, and Doctor Merryman."

Jonathan Swift

Irish clergyman and author
(Quoting a medieval Latin poem)

"Half of the confusion in the world comes from not knowing how little we need. I live more simply now, and with more peace."

Richard E Byrd

Naval officer and polar explorer

"It's hard for me to tell whether it's my age or the stroke I had two years ago that's at the root of what I'm feeling now at fifty-one. My stroke really aged me. I walked in the golden clouds, and there's nothing like that for perspective. Before my stroke, I was stuck in the everyday whirl, just coping with life. I was running like a hamster on a wheel. Now my focus is on the beauty of every day. And I love that."

Marcia LaFond
Jewelry artist

Life

"Life is a great big canvas, and you should
throw all the paint on it you can."

Danny Kaye
Entertainer

"Life is what we are alive to. It is not length but breadth. To be alive only to appetite, pleasure, pride, money-making, and not to goodness, kindness, purity, love, history, poetry, music, flowers, stars, God, and eternal hope is to be all but dead."

Maltbie D. Babcock
Minister and hymn writer

"You know, by the time you reach my age, you've made plenty of mistakes if you've lived your life properly."

Ronald Reagan

40th President of the United States

"A human life is a story touched by God."

Hans Christian Andersen

Danish author

"Late on the third day, at the very moment when at sunset, we were making our way through a herd of hippopotamuses, there flashed upon my mind—unforeseen and unsought—the phrase, 'Reverence for life.'"

Albert Schweitzer

French-German theologian and humanitarian

"Life is like a good pizza.
Even when it's bad it's good."

Paula Devicq

Actress

"The aim of life is to live, and to live means to be aware, joyously, drunkenly, serenely, divinely aware."

Henry Miller
Novelist

"A happy life is made up of little things—a gift sent, a letter written, a call made, a recommendation given, transportation provided, a cake made, a book lent, a check sent."

Carol Holmes

Author

"No one ever went to their deathbed saying,
'You know, I wish I'd eaten more rice cakes.'"

Amy Krouse Rosenthal

Children's author and radio host

"I like living. I have sometimes been wildly, despairingly, acutely miserable, racked with sorrow, but through it all I still know quite certainly that just to be alive is a good thing."

Agatha Christie
Mystery writer

"Any day above ground is a good day."

Anonymous

"Now, as I approach my eighty-fourth year, I find it interesting to reflect on what has made my life, even with its moments of pain, such an essentially happy one. I have come to the conclusion that the most important element of human life is faith. If God were to take away all His blessings: health, physical fitness, wealth, intelligence, and leave me but one gift, I would ask for faith. For with faith in Him, in his goodness, mercy, love for me and belief in everlasting life, I believe I could suffer the loss of all other gifts and still be happy, trustful, leaving all to His inscrutable Providence."

Rose Fitzgerald Kennedy
Philanthropist and matriarch of the Kennedy family

"We live in deeds, not years:
in thoughts, not breaths;
In feelings, not in figures on a dial.
We should count time by heart-throbs.
He most lives who thinks most,
feels the noblest, acts the best."

Philip James Bailey

Poet

"What is life? It is the flash of a firefly in the night. It is the breath of the buffalo in the wintertime. It is the little shadow which runs across the grass and loses itself in the sunset."

Crowfoot

Chief and warrior of the Siksika First Nation

"Everything happening, great and small, is a parable whereby God speaks to us, and the art of life is to get the message."

Malcolm Muggeridge

Journalist

"Life is like a ten-speed bicycle.
Most of us have gears we never use."

Charles M. Schulz

Cartoonist

"Variety's the very spice of life,
that gives it all its flavor"

William Cowper

Poet

"Life is too short to drink the house wine."

Helen Thomas

White House correspondent

"Considering the alternative,
it's not too bad at all."

Maurice Chevalier

French actor and cabaret singer
(When asked, "How do you feel about being elderly?")

"There is nothing in the world, I venture to say, that would so effectively help one to survive even the worst conditions, as the knowledge that there is a meaning in one's life."

Viktor Frankl

Austrian psychiatrist and Holocaust survivor

Change

"The art of life lies in a constant
readjustment to our surroundings."

Okakura Kakuzo

Japanese author

"The survival of the fittest is the ageless law of nature, but the fittest are rarely the strong. The fittest are those endowed with the qualifications for adaptation, the ability to accept the inevitable and conform to the unavoidable, to harmonize with existing or changing conditions."

Dave E. Smalley
Author

"Life is not always what one wants it to be, but to make the best of it as it is, is the only way of being happy."

Jennie Churchill

American-born British socialite and mother of Winston Churchill

"Suffering is traumatic and awful and we get angry and we shake our fists at the heavens and we weep. But in the process we discover a new tomorrow, one we never would have imagined otherwise."

Rob Bell

Author and motivational speaker

"Very often a change of self is needed more than a change of scene."

Arthur Christopher Benson

British academic

"Change can be scary but you know what's scarier? Allowing fear to stop you from growing, evolving, and progressing."

Mandy Hale

Author and blogger

"An oak and a reed were arguing about their strength when a strong wind came up. The reed avoided being uprooted by bending and leaning with the gusts of wind. But the oak stood firm and was torn up by the roots."

Aesop
Greek fabulist

"When you cannot do what you have always done, then you only do what matters most."

Robert D. Hales

Businessman and leader in the
Church of Jesus Christ of Latter-Day Saints

Courage & Hope

"Start by doing what's necessary, then do what's possible, and suddenly you are doing the impossible."

St. Francis of Assisi

"We must make the best of those
ills which cannot be avoided."

Alexander Hamilton

American founding father

"Ofttimes the test of courage becomes
rather to live than to die."

Vittorio Alfieri
Italian dramatist

"I learned that courage was not the absence of fear, but the triumph over it. The brave man is not he who does not feel afraid, but he who conquers that fear."

Nelson Mandela
President of South Africa

"Accept that all of us can be hurt, that all of us can — and surely will at times — fail. Other vulnerabilities, like being embarrassed or risking love, can be terrifying too. I think we should follow a simple rule: If we can take the worst, take the risk."

Dr. Joyce Brothers
Popular psychologist

"You gain strength, courage, and confidence by each experience in which you really stop to look fear in the face. You are able to say to yourself, 'I have lived through this horror. I can take the next thing that comes along.'"

Eleanor Roosevelt
First Lady and social activist

"Toughness is in the soul and
spirit, not in the muscles."

Alex Karras

Professional football player and actor

"The greatest test of courage on earth is to bear defeat without losing heart."

Robert Green Ingersoll

Political organizer, attorney, and secular humanist writer

"In the central place of every heart there is a recording chamber. So long as it receives a message of beauty, hope, cheer, and courage— so long you are young. When the wires are all down and our heart is covered with the snow of pessimism and the ice of cynicism, then, and only then, are you grown old."

Douglas MacArthur
General

"A woman is like a tea bag. You never know how strong she is until she gets in hot water."

Eleanor Roosevelt

First Lady and social activist

"Without courage, all other
virtues lose their meaning."

Winston Churchill
Prime Minister of the United Kingdom

"Anyone who is among the living has hope."

Ecclesiastes 9:4

"The fishermen know that the sea is dangerous and the storm terrible, but they have never found these dangers sufficient reason for remaining ashore."

Vincent van Gogh
Dutch Post-Impressionist painter

"Hope is a good thing—maybe the best thing, and no good thing ever dies."

Stephen King
Author

Reflection

"Reflect upon your present blessings, of which every man has many; not on your past misfortune, of which all men have some."

Charles Dickens

Author

"You have the capacity to choose what you think about. If you choose to think about past hurts, you will continue to feel bad. While it's true that you can't change the effect past influences had on you once, you can change the effect they have on you now."

Gary McKay

Psychologist and author of parenting books

"Old age is like climbing a mountain. You climb from ledge to ledge. The higher you get, the more tired you become, but your view becomes much more extensive."

Ingmar Bergman
Swedish film director

"When parents say to kids, 'Go to your room and think about what you've done,' it's really good practice for what you do every night as an adult."

Pat Tobin
Animator

"The longest journey
Is the journey inwards
Of him who has chosen his destiny
Who has started upon his quest
For the source of his being."

Dag Hammarskjöld
First Secretary General of the United Nations

"The roots of all our lives go very, very deep, and we can't really understand a person unless we have the chance of knowing who that person has been, and what that person has done, and liked and suffered and believed."

"What's been important in my understanding of myself and others is the fact that each one of us is so much more than any one thing. A sick child is much more than his or her sickness. A person with a disability is much, much more than a handicap. A pediatrician is more than a medical doctor. You're much more than your job description, your age, your income, or your output."

Fred Rogers
Children's show host

"As a white candle
In a holy place,
So is the beauty
Of an aged face."

Joseph Campbell

Mythology and comparative religion author

"Recall it as often as you wish, a happy memory never wears out."

Anonymous

"The most important trip you may take
in life is meeting people halfway"

Henry Boye
Author

"Failures are like skinned knees—
painful but superficial."

H. Ross Perot

Businessman and politician

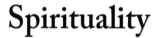

Spirituality

"What the caterpillar calls the end of the world, the master calls the butterfly."

Richard Bach

Writer

"How often we look upon God as our last and feeblest resource! We go to Him because we have nowhere else to go. And then we learn that the storms of life have driven us, not upon the rocks, but into the desired haven."

George MacDonald

Methodist missionary

"God brings no man into the conflicts of life to desert him. Every man has a friend in heaven whose resources are unlimited: And on Him we may call at any hour and find sympathy and assistance."

John Hill Aughey
Author

"Listen to God with a broken heart. He is not only the one who mends it, but also the Father who wipes away the tears."

Kriss Jami

Poet

"I question every presumption we have about human potential. Do we have to age like everybody else? I don't believe so. Our biological age, our spiritual age, are different things."

Deepak Chopra

Author and alternative medicine advocate

"Learn to get in touch with silence within yourself and know that everything in life has a purpose."

Elizabeth Kübler-Ross

Psychiatrist and creator of the "Five Stages of Grief" model

"Never forget the three powerful resources you always have available to you: love, prayer, and forgiveness."

H. Jackson Brown, Jr.
Author

"What I learned at a very early age was that I was responsible for my life. And as I became more spiritually conscious, I learned that we are all responsible for ourselves, that you create your own reality by the way you think and therefore act. You cannot blame apartheid, your parents, your circumstances, because you are not your circumstances. You are your possibilities. If you know that, you can do anything."

Oprah Winfrey
Television host, businesswoman, and philanthropist

"The best remedy for those who are afraid, lonely, or unhappy is to go outside, somewhere where they can be quiet, alone with the heavens, nature and God. Because only then does one feel that all is as it should be."

Anne Frank

Diarist and victim of the Holocaust

"Have courage for the great sorrows of life and patience for the small ones; and when you have laboriously accomplished your daily task, go to sleep in peace. God is awake."

Victor Hugo
French novelist

"To what greater inspiration and counsel can we turn than to the imperishable truth to be found in this treasure house, the Bible?"

Queen Elizabeth II

"I find the great thing in this world is not so much where we stand, as in what direction we are moving. To reach the port of heaven, we must sometimes sail with the wind, and sometimes against it; but we must sail and not drift, nor lie at anchor."

Oliver Wendell Holmes, Sr.

Poet, physician, and essayist

"God answers all the prayers. Sometimes He answers 'yes,' sometimes He answers 'no,' and sometimes the answer is, 'you gotta be kidding.'"

Jimmy Carter

37th President of the United States

"God hath not promised skies always blue,
Flower-strewn pathways all our lives through;
God hath not promised sun without rain,
Joy without sorrow, peace without pain.
But God hath promised strength for the day,
Rest for the labor, light for the way;
Grace for the trials, help from above,
Unfailing sympathy, undying love."

Annie Johnson Flint
Author and poet

"Faith is taking the first step even when you don't see the whole staircase."

Dr. Martin Luther King, Jr.
Minister and civil rights leader

"Let gratitude be the pillow upon which you kneel to say your nightly prayer. And let faith be the bridge you build to overcome evil and welcome good."

Maya Angelou

Writer and civil rights activist

End of Life

"The Lord is near to the brokenhearted,
and saves the crushed in spirit."

Psalm 34:18

"No, I do not worry about death because I know that the minute the man upstairs wants me, I'm His."

Paul McCartney

Musician

"Every human being's life is a story, a unique story that nobody ever lived before and no one will ever live again. When we learn to think of life as a story, then we can come to think of death not as punishment but as punctuation.

What we want to know about a book or movie is not how long it is, but how good it is, and we can learn to think of life in the same way. If life is a story, then we understand it better as we get closer to the end.

Only then can we understand the real significance of something that happened back in chapter three or four.

If life is a story, we can wish it would go on forever, but we understand that even the best of stories has to end. It would be a strange story if it did go on forever.

So instead of grieving that it has to end, we can feel blessed that we were lucky enough to have been a part of it."

Harold S. Kushner

Rabbi

"Death happens, despite what we do to avoid it. Everything that begins, ends. The fact may not be welcome, but it is realistic. Death is a central part of life and despite everything it takes from us, so too it enriches and strengthens."

Edward S. Gleason

Episcopal minister and author

"The experience of dying frequently includes glimpses of another world and those waiting in it. Although they provide few details, dying people speak with awe and wonder of the presence of people whom we cannot see — perhaps people they have known and loved. They know, often without being told, that they are dying, and may even tell us when their deaths will occur."

Maggie Callanan & Patricia Kelley
Hospice nurses and authors of "Final Gifts"

"The work of the dying is theirs, not ours. Ours is to travel alongside, as companions on their journey."

Penelope Wilcock

Author, hospice chaplain, and Methodist minister

"I started talking. I told him about my visit with Lisa and the new baby. And I talked about our other grandchildren. How dear they all were to us. How well they were developing…I talked about our courtship and the long years of waiting before we could get married and how young we had been. I talked about the farm and the good times we had there.

I talked for hours. Talked about the silly things, the good things, the times that I had cherished, about everything that had been important to me in our life together. I held his hand and poured my heart out. I told him over and over again how much I loved him and how happy he had always made me."

Dr. Joyce Brothers

Popular psychologist
(Describing her last hours with her husband)

"Even when the end is in sight, the dying have a need to hope. Regardless of whether or not we think that hope is valid, it is something we should protect. Hope should never go away, but what we hope for can change. First, we may hope to recover; then we may hope for a peaceful death. We may hope that the children will be alright, and we may hope that there is a heaven.

Hope and reality needn't clash. You don't have to tell lies to keep hope alive. I've sat with hundreds of people who were in their last days, hours, or minutes, and I never once said, 'There is no hope.'"

David Kessler
Author, "The Needs of the Dying"

"Parents continue to live within us in our memories, our attitudes, even in our gestures and mannerisms. As time passes, the initial pain and confusion of mourning lessens; a deeper, wiser understanding emerges."

Marc D. Angel
Rabbi

"A sick man turned to his doctor as he was leaving the examination room and said, 'Doctor, I am afraid to die. Tell me what lies on the other side.' Very quietly, the doctor said, 'I don't know.'

'You don't know? You, a God-fearing man, do not know what is on the other side?'

The doctor was holding the handle of the door; on the other side came a sound of scratching and whining, and as he opened the door, a dog sprang into the room and leaped on him with an eager show of gladness.

Turning to the patient, the doctor said, 'Did you notice my dog? He's never been in this room before. He didn't know what was inside. He knew nothing except that his master was here, and when the door opened, he sprang in without fear.

I know little of what is on the other side of death, but I do know one thing: I know God is there and that is enough.'"

Anonymous

Important things to say when visiting a
friend or a loved one who is terminally ill:

"Please forgive me,"
"I forgive you,"
"Thank you,"
"I love you."

Ira Bysock

Physician and author of
"The Four Things That Matter Most"

"There comes a moment when we all must realize that life is short and in the end the only thing that really counts is not how others see us, but how God sees us."

Billy Graham
Minister and evangelist

"I used to imagine that my father had left me a
letter, or a series of letters that would be
delivered at key junctures of my life. I still hold
out hope that one will show up"

Anderson Cooper
Television journalist

"If only you could imagine
The wonders of this place
Where every day I look upon
The glory of God's face.
I sing the song of angels
As I walk the streets of gold
And hear the saints recounting
The greatest stories ever told.
Heaven is everything
We've dreamed;
This life is not the end,
And my love is with you always
Until we meet again."

R. Fogle

"May the Lord bless you all the days of your life, and may you live to see your children's children."

Psalm 128:5-6

Each of us is in charge of our own life.

Make the most of yours!

Don't let your spirit grow old!